## 1. Introduction

Intellectual property disputes between actual or potential horizontal competitors are an unavoidable consequence of the uncertain nature of the property right that a patent represents.[1] The parties involved in such disputes can choose to litigate their cases to a final conclusion, but they may also resolve their disagreements with settlements. Such settlements can produce a variety of benefits, including lower social and private litigation costs, faster entry by new producers, and the reduction of risk. Yet such settlements can also raise antitrust concerns, since they are agreements between firms that are, at least with some probability, direct competitors.

Some kinds of patent dispute settlements clearly raise more concerns than others. A cash payment from an incumbent firm to a potentially infringing entrant in exchange for the entrant's commitment to abandon or delay the marketing of its product would clearly be worrisome; consumers would probably prefer the firms to litigate rather than reach such a settlement.[2] A royalty-bearing license that enabled an entrant to immediately market its product might raise fewer red flags; such a settlement could conceivably benefit both consumers and the parties to the settlement agreement. In a related paper (Schrag (2004)), I demonstrate some of the difficulties that can arise in an analysis of the competitive effects of this kind of agreement.

In this paper, I analyze the effects of a particular kind of patent dispute settlement between potential horizontal competitors, namely a royalty-free license in exchange for delayed

---

[1] See Shapiro and Lemley (2005) for a discussion of the "probabilistic" nature of intellectual property rights. As they point out, a patent is not an iron-clad right to exclude a competitor. It is instead a right to try to exclude a competitor.

[2] The Federal Trade Commission has challenged patent settlements between Schering-Plough and two potential generic competitors, Upsher-Smith Laboratories and the ESI Lederle unit of American Home Products, on the grounds that Schering had essentially paid its rivals not to compete. See http://www.ftc.gov/os/2001/04/scheringpart3cmp.pdf. In December, 2003, the Commission released its final decision in this case, finding that the agreements were anticompetitive. See *In the Matter of Schering Plough Corporation, et al.,* Dkt No. 9297 (December 18, 2003) (final decision of the Commission). In March 2005 the 11th Circuit Court of Appeals reversed the FTC's decision. For related examples in the pharmaceutical industry, see also *Abbott Labs.,* Dkt. No. C-3945 (May 22, 2000) (consent order); *Geneva Pharm., Inc.,* Dkt. No. C-3946 (May 22, 2000) (consent order) and *Hoechst Marion Roussel, Inc.,* Dkt. No 9293 (May 8, 2001) (consent order).

entry by the potentially infringing firm.   I assume that, aside from the license, the incumbent

cannot transfer to the entrant any other net consideration, e.g. cash.  Under this assumption, the

Federal Trade Commission's concern about an incumbent paying for delayed entry that was the

focus of its recent *Schering* case cannot arise.[3]  The central question that I address is whether such

settlements for "time off the patent" serve consumers' interests.  Given a choice, would

consumers accept such settlements, or would they prefer that the parties litigate their cases?  My

main finding is that royalty-free licenses for delayed entry do not necessarily serve consumers'

interests, even if the entrants have all of the bargaining power in their negotiations with

incumbent patent-holders and can therefore obtain relatively early entry dates through their

settlements.

It may seem that a patent settlement that licensed the entrant to come into the market after

a mutually agreeable delay would tend to be competitively neutral, as long as the litigants'

bargaining was not distorted by a cash payment from the incumbent to the entrant.  If litigation

costs are small, it is plausible that such a settlement would more or less reflect the expected

outcome of the trial, and consumers would therefore be approximately indifferent between

litigation and settlement, at least as long as their discount rate was not very different from the

litigants' discount rates.  Suppose, for instance, that a patent-holder's chance of winning an

infringement case against a potential competitor is fifty percent.  If the remaining life of the

patent were ten years and litigation costs were small, an agreement that licensed the potentially

infringing firm to enter in approximately five years would essentially reflect the expected

outcome of the trial.  Setting aside the issue of discounting, such a settlement at first glance seems

both reasonable and likely.  If the entrant tried to obtain a significantly earlier entry date through

the settlement, the incumbent should have an incentive to litigate rather than settle.  If the

incumbent tried to obtain a significantly later entry date through the settlement, the entrant would

---

[3] See the discussion in note 2.

have an incentive to litigate rather than settle. Under both litigation and the hypothesized settlement for time off the relevant patent's life, then, the entrant would expect to be in the market — and consumers would expect to benefit from the entrant's presence — for approximately five years.

In order to test this argument, I develop a formal model in which two entrants each decide whether or not to develop a substitute product in order to challenge an incumbent firm's patent-protected monopoly in some market. After an entrant successfully develops a product, the incumbent can sue for patent infringement, and the firms can either litigate their case or settle for a royalty-free license that permits the entrant to sell its product after some delay. Even though I assume that litigation is costless, I show that a settlement between the incumbent and the entrant that develops its product first creates a non-negative surplus that they can divide. This surplus arises because their settlement discourages the trailing entrant's product development, increasing the profits that the incumbent and the leading entrant can share. The incumbent and the entrant that develops a product first therefore strictly prefer settlement to litigation, even in the absence of direct litigation costs. In order to identify the effects of the firms' settlements, I analyze consumer welfare and the entrants' product development decisions both when the firms can settle their cases and when the firms always litigate any patent infringement cases.

In the model, the relevant market is a natural duopoly, so at most one entrant completes its project. Under this assumption, I find that settlements for time off the patent generally leave consumers worse off than they would be if the firms litigated their cases. This conclusion does not change even if the terms of settlement are very favorable to the potential entrants, whose interests during settlement negotiations are to some degree aligned with consumers' interests; both consumers and entrants prefer earlier entry, *ceteris paribus*. My formal assumption about settlement bargaining is that the incumbent captures none of the surplus from avoiding trial, so any entry occurs at the earliest possible date that is consistent with the incumbent being willing to settle rather than litigate.

My analysis reveals two reasons that settlements can harm consumers' interests. First, the time that consumers expect to benefit from a *particular* entrant represents a lower bound on the expected time that consumers would benefit from *some* entrant. For example, a particular entrant may have a fifty-fifty chance of winning an infringement case, but a settlement that enables the entrant to sell its product halfway through the remaining patent life could shortchange consumers, because another entrant may emerge if the first loses its infringement case. Given this possibility, consumers would have a greater than fifty-fifty chance of benefiting from *some* entrant. I develop this argument more fully in the example in the next section.

Second, the form of patent settlement that I analyze can undermine the entrants' incentives to invent around the incumbent's patent. If the entrant that completes its product development first always settles with the incumbent, a slower entrant would likely never have a chance to earn duopoly profits.[4] If the entrant that completes its product development first always litigates, meanwhile, a slower entrant would possibly have an opportunity to earn duopoly profits, because the first entrant may lose its patent infringement case. The prospect of settlement thus increases the relative importance to an entrant of being the first to develop a competing product and, therefore, discourages an entrant from undertaking a project that it believes will take a long time to complete.

It would be wrong to conclude from the results that the settlement of intellectual property disputes generally harm consumer welfare. First, the analysis considers only one kind of settlement that parties to such a dispute could reach. Second, in order to expose the basic arguments more clearly, the analysis abstracts away from key factors, such as the private and social costs of litigation. Incorporating these costs into the model would tend to make settlement look more socially desirable. Of course, the analysis also abstracts away from some of the social

---

[4] The first entrant and the incumbent could always guarantee that the later entrant did not receive duopoly profits by including in their settlement agreement a provision for the first entrant's immediate entry if any other firm could enter. Then the second entrant would not earn duopoly profits even if it won an infringement case before the first entrant's negotiated entry date.

4

benefits of litigation. For example, litigating a patent infringement or invalidity case reveals valuable information about the true scope or even existence of the patent-holder's property right. Incorporating such benefits into the model would tend to make litigation look more socially desirable.

The formal analysis does, however, support two broad conclusions. First, the model highlights the importance of analyzing the effects of any patent settlement on the incentives of the relevant third parties before drawing any conclusions about the settlement's effect on consumers' interests. If an incumbent monopolist and the first entrant to challenge the incumbent's monopoly craft an agreement that, intentionally or not, undermines other firms' incentives to develop competing products, consumers may be worse off than they would be if the firms litigated their case. I develop this idea further in Schrag (2004), in which I examine the competitive effects of a patent dispute settlement in which the incumbent grants the entrant an immediate-entry, royalty-bearing license.

Second, because the model reveals that patent settlements that license entry at a date that is consistent with the expected outcome of the trial are not necessarily beneficial to consumers, it suggests that other settlement terms that help parties reach agreement on a delayed entry license cannot be assumed to be ancillary to a pro-competitive outcome. If these other terms raise independent competition concerns, a settlement is even less likely to benefit consumers and should therefore be subject to even greater scrutiny. For example, suppose that two firms settled for a royalty-free delayed entry license, along with a side deal that transferred intellectual property from the entrant to the incumbent in exchange for cash. An outside observer might worry that the incumbent was tempted to overpay for the intellectual property in order to convince the entrant to accept a relatively late entry date.[5] The parties might argue that such a side deal was necessary in order to achieve any agreement at all, and that, furthermore, the

---

[5] This was the FTC's contention in its *Schering* case; see note 2, *supra*.

negotiated entry date simply reflected the expected outcome of the trial that they avoided, meaning that the entrant would compete for the same amount of time, in expectation. For a variety of reasons, third parties may not be in a position to evaluate whether the negotiated entry date actually was consistent with the expected outcome of the case.[6] My findings suggest that, even if the negotiated entry date actually did reflect the expected outcome of the case, consumers might very well have been better off anyway if the parties had litigated.

There is a small economic literature on the antitrust issues that patent settlements raise. Shapiro (2003) proposes that a settlement of an intellectual property dispute, including a settlement for a license that permits delayed entry by a potential entrant, should satisfy a simple rule to pass antitrust muster, namely that expected consumer surplus must be at least as large under the settlement as under continued litigation. In practice, such a standard would often be difficult to implement, because it would often involve a highly subjective analysis of the likely outcome of the parties' litigation. Shapiro argues that there always exists a settlement that leaves both the parties and consumers better off than they would be with litigation, but he does not analyze the effect of patent settlements on third parties' incentives to develop products.[7]

Meurer (1989) studies the effect of antitrust policy on patent settlements when the patent holder has private information about its patent's validity and can make a take-it-or-leave-it offer to a competitor. In his model, antitrust policy falls on a continuum between what he terms a laissez-faire and a lump sum policy. A laissez-faire policy enables the two parties to split monopoly profits, while a lump-sum policy limits the parties to a split of the Cournot-Nash profits in any settlement they reach. He finds that antitrust policy has no effect on the probability

---

[6] In such a situation, the defendants in the antitrust case would have a natural incentive to exaggerate the strength of the incumbent's case in the underlying patent case, since that would tend to reduce their antitrust liability. See the discussion in O'Rourke and Brodley (2003). Evidence that could overcome this exaggeration may often be protected by attorney-client privilege.

[7] Shapiro does, however, endorse the FTC's concern about delayed entry patent settlements that include cash payments from the incumbent to the alleged infringer. See also Shapiro and Lemley (2004) and Hovenkamp et al. (2003).

that the parties settle. In the equilibrium of his signaling model, a patent holder that holds a valid patent always refuses to settle, and a patent holder with an invalid patent must also refuse to settle with a high enough probability that the competitor is willing to litigate in the event that the patent holder refuses to settle. The competitor's payoff from litigation is unaffected by antitrust policy, because if it loses its case it earns nothing, while it enters as a duopolist if it wins. But then the patent holder's settlement behavior must also be unaffected by antitrust policy, in order to satisfy the equilibrium condition that the competitor is indifferent between settling and litigating, regardless of the antitrust policy. Meurer focuses only on the issue of patent invalidity, so he does not consider the effect of settlement on a potential competitor's incentive to invent around the incumbent's patent.

In a related paper that examines potential entrants' investment incentives, Choi (1998) analyzes the effects of litigation over a patent's validity when there are multiple potential entrants. He shows that the information externalities associated with litigation can cause the entrants to play a waiting game, in which each entrant may delay their entry (and the ensuing patent litigation) in order to increase the chance that its rival goes first and bears the cost of testing the validity of the incumbent firm's patent. He also shows that the patent holder may have an incentive to delay a patent suit against the first entrant to present itself as a potential infringer, since doing so eliminates the possibility that the second entrant could benefit from information revealed by the first entrant's litigation. Choi does not consider the possibility that the entrants will settle their patent litigation.

In the next section I present a simple example that illustrates the basic idea that underlies the formal model, which I introduce in section three. Section four concludes.

## 2.    An Example

Consider a market that will last for ten years, and assume that there is no discounting. One risk neutral incumbent is already selling in the market, and there are two risk neutral and identical potential entrants. The first entrant's product is ready for immediate sale, but the second entrant's product will not be available for two years, either because it requires additional development or because it must obtain regulatory approval. I assume that the second entrant's incremental cost of bringing its product to market is sufficiently high that it finds entry as the third supplier to be unprofitable. If the first entrant successfully launches its product, therefore, the second entrant stops work on its product and does not enter.

Each entrant's product potentially infringes a patent that the incumbent holds. Suppose that each entrant has a fifty percent chance of prevailing in court if the incumbent sues for infringement, and suppose further that the entrants' cases are independent. To simplify the example and expose the basic argument, I assume that both patent litigation and any settlement negotiations are instantaneous and costless. It follows from these assumptions that the incumbent will immediately sue for patent infringement if an entrant launches its product, and the parties will either settle their case or litigate.

Rather than imposing a particular structure to the settlement bargaining, I analyze how the expected outcome of the litigation influences the range of possible settlements that could arise. I assume that a settlement consists of an entry date and, in the case of the first entrant, a provision that it can enter the market in the event that the second entrant is able to sell its product. Such a provision would always serve the interests of both the incumbent and the first entrant, since it would discourage the second entrant from continuing its product development following a settlement between the incumbent and the first entrant.

Under the model's assumptions, the incumbent and the *second* entrant are indifferent between settling and litigating.[8] In the absence of either litigation costs or risk aversion, a settlement between the incumbent and the second entrant creates no surplus to divide, so the terms of any agreement would exactly reflect the expected outcome of their litigation. When the incumbent and the *first* entrant settle, however, they do create and therefore may divide a non-negative surplus. The source of this surplus is the entry-deterring effect of the settlement on the second entrant's investment. Define $\pi_E > 0$ as the yearly profit that the entrant earns from selling its product. Define $\pi_M$ and $\pi_D$ as the incumbent's yearly profit as a monopolist and a duopolist, respectively, and assume that $\pi_M > \pi_D > 0$. If the first entrant and the incumbent fail to settle their dispute before trial, then their payoffs are determined by the expected outcome of their litigation:

First Entrant's Litigation Payoff $= L_E = 0.5(10)\pi_E = 5\pi_E,$

Incumbent's Litigation Payoff $= L_I$

$$= 0.5(10)\pi_D + 0.5[0.5(10)\pi_M + 0.5(2\pi_M + 8\pi_D)]$$

$$= 3\pi_M + 7\pi_D.$$

The entrant's payoff reflects the fact that it has a fifty percent chance of winning a 10- year duopoly and a fifty percent chance of winning nothing. The incumbent's payoff reflects the fact that it has a fifty percent chance of prevailing in its litigation against the first incumbent, in which case it still faces the prospect of possible entry from the second incumbent.

Given these litigation payoffs, it is clear that, irrespective of the exact nature of settlement bargaining, the incumbent will not agree to a settlement that enables the entrant to compete for more than seven years, and the first entrant will not agree to a settlement that allows it to compete for less than five years. Both parties strictly prefer a settlement that permits competition for between five and seven years over the alternative of litigating. The exact terms

---

[8] This would not necessarily be true if the litigants could settle for an immediate entry, royalty bearing license.

of any settlement in this range would presumably depend on the parties' relative bargaining power.

The example illustrates how, even in the absence of risk aversion or litigation costs, settlement can still be advantageous for the incumbent and the first entrant. By causing the second entrant to abandon its entry plans, the settlement between the incumbent and the first entrant increases the total profits that they can split. If the first entrant receives any of the surplus that the settlement creates, its entry date under settlement will be earlier than its expected entry date under litigation, possibly leading to the conclusion that the settlement benefits consumers. Such a conclusion may not be valid, as the following analysis of consumers' interests illustrates.

Were settlement between the incumbent and the entrants impossible, consumers would face a fifty percent chance of ten years of duopoly (the first entrant wins its infringement case), a twenty-five percent chance of ten years of monopoly (both entrants lose their cases), and a twenty-five percent chance of two years of monopoly followed by eight years of duopoly (the first entrant loses and the second entrant wins). Define $CS_n$ as the (time-invariant) yearly consumer surplus when $n \in \{1, 2\}$ firms are selling in the market. Consumers' expected surplus if the entrants always litigate their cases is:

$$ECS_{lit} = 0.5(10CS_2) + 0.25(10CS_1) + 0.25(2CS_1 + 8CS_2) = 3CS_1 + 7CS_2.$$

Consumers' expected surplus under a settlement that permits the first entrant to compete for $t^*$ years is

$$ECS_{settle} = (10 - t^*)CS_1 + t^*CS_2.$$

Because $CS_2 > CS_1$, consumers strictly prefer settlement to litigation if and only if $t^* > 7$, but the preceding analysis of the litigants' incentives indicates that the incumbent would not be willing to accept such a settlement. If the incumbent has any bargaining power at all, i.e. if it captures any of the bargaining surplus, then under a settlement the first entrant would compete for less than seven years and consumers would then be strictly worse off if the entrants and the incumbent settle rather than litigate.

The example illustrates how the settlement of patent litigation between the incumbent firm and an entrant can harm consumers' interests, even if the settlement allows the entrant to enter the market sooner than the date that would reflect the strength of its infringement case. A simple rule of thumb that consumers will be indifferent between litigation and a settlement that reflects the expected outcome of the trial fails to recognize that, if the settling entrant were to lose its infringement case, another entrant may replace it.[9] From the perspective of consumers, the probability that the first entrant prevails in its infringement case is a lower bound on the probability that they will benefit from *some* entrant. If the incumbent and the first entrant can craft a settlement that discourages subsequent entrants from developing and offering a product, consumers may strongly prefer litigation to settlement.

The first entrant clearly benefits when it receives a share of the surplus created by deterring the second entrant's possible entry. This increase in the first entrant's profits may strengthen its *ex ante* incentive to develop a product and challenge the incumbent's monopoly. On the other hand, the second entrant is clearly hurt by the settlement between the incumbent and the first entrant, and the decrease in the second entrant's profits may weaken the early incentive to develop a product. The net effect of settlement on the entrants' initial incentives to develop products (before it is known which will be first and which will be second) is not immediately obvious. I explore this issue in more detail in the formal model in the next section.

---

[9] Willig and Bigelow (2002, p. 2) seem to suggest just such a rule of thumb. Their paper does not address the effect of patent settlements on third party investment behavior.

## 3.    A Model of Patent Litigation Settlement

Consider a market in which an incumbent firm is currently selling a product. Because it holds a patent that claims its product, the incumbent initially faces no competition. I normalize the patent life to unity and assume for simplicity that there is no discounting.[10] I also assume that free entry immediately drives profits to zero after the patent expires. Before that occurs, two potential entrants can each attempt to invent around the incumbent's patent and enter early. I index the entrants by $i \in \{a, b\}$. In order to model the entrants' product development decisions, I assume that each entrant can begin a development project at time $t = 0$. To simplify the model, I assume that this is the only time at which an entrant can start a project.[11] Associated with entrant $i$'s project is a parameter $z_i$ that represents the amount of time the entrant would need to complete the project. I assume that $z_a$ and $z_b$ are random variables that are independently and identically distributed on the support $[0, \infty)$ according to the continuous probability distribution function $f(\cdot)$. Entrant $i$ knows how long its own project will take, i.e. entrant $i$ observes $z_i$ at time 0, but neither entrant can observe how long the other entrant's project will take. While each entrant knows when its rival has completed its project, neither entrant can observe whether its rival is working on an unfinished project. Each entrant must therefore decide whether to continue investing in its project without knowing what its rival is doing. If an entrant decides to pursue a project, it must pay a flow cost $c > 0$ until it either completes or abandons the project.

To streamline the exposition that follows, I often refer to the "first entrant" and the "second entrant." By definition, the first entrant's project has the earlier completion date, and the second entrant's project has the later completion date. Of course, the identities of the first and

---

[10] Incorporating discounting into the model is straightforward, but it complicates the presentation without adding additional insights.

[11] Relaxing this assumption would enable an entrant to choose a more complicated investment strategy, since it could defer a decision about whether to start a project until after it knew whether its rival would quickly complete its project. I conjecture that the main qualitative conclusions of the paper would continue to hold even if this sort of behavior were possible.

second entrant are not known *ex ante*; either entrant *a* or entrant *b* could have the fastest project. The distributions of the first and second entrants' project completion dates are the well-known distributions of the first and second order statistics.

The firms' flow profits at any point in time depend on the number of firms that are in the market. If there are $n \in \{1, 2, \ldots\}$ firms in the market, the incumbent earns $\pi_I(n)$, and any entrant that is selling earns $\pi_E(n)$. It is reasonable to assume that $\pi_x(n) > \pi_x(n + 1)$, $x \in \{I, E\}$; additional entry reduces the firms' flow profits. I initially simplify the model by assuming that $\pi_E(2) > \pi_E(3) = 0$. This assumption means that the second entrant will abandon its product development if the first entrant to complete a project successfully enters. The second entrant has no incentive to incur development costs if it anticipates earning no profit from selling its product.[12]

After an entrant completes a project, the incumbent can sue for patent infringement, in which case the parties either litigate the case or settle. Each entrant wins its case with probability $\alpha > 0$, and the two entrants' cases are independent. As in the example, I assume that both litigation and settlement are instantaneous and costless, in which case the incumbent always sues when an entrant completes its project. While strong, this assumption permits me to focus on the incumbent and first entrant's ability to extract rents from the second entrant. In the conclusion I discuss the potential effect of relaxing this assumption. A settlement of any infringement litigation between the incumbent and an entrant consists of an entry date and, in the case of the first entrant to complete its project, a provision that it can enter the market in the event that the second entrant is able to sell its product. As explained in the previous section, such a provision discourages the remaining entrant from developing a product once one of the entrants has finished its product and settled with the incumbent, so such a provision would always serve the joint interests of the incumbent and the first entrant.

---

[12] The assumption that $\pi_E(2) > \pi_E(3) = 0$ is consistent with a model in which the entrants' products are perfect substitutes for each other, and they engage in Bertrand price competition. In such a model, neither entrant would earn a positive flow profit if they both entered.

In order to establish a benchmark, I first analyze the entrants' product development decisions when the incumbent and the entrants are not permitted to settle their legal disputes and instead must litigate. The timing of the model is as follows. First, each entrant $i$ chooses a "cutoff" project, say $\bar{z}_i$, $i \in \{a, b\}$. Next, each entrant learns the amount of time it would take to complete its project, i.e. entrant $i$ observes the realization of $z_i$. Entrant $i$ then pursues any project with a completion date $z_i \leq \bar{z}_i$ until either it completes the project or its rival prevails in patent infringement litigation with the incumbent, whichever is earlier. A pure strategy Nash equilibrium is a pair of cutoff projects, say $(\bar{z}_a^*, \bar{z}_b^*)$, such that each entrant's choice of a cutoff project maximizes its expected profits given the other entrant's strategy. In the following Proposition, I describe the unique pure strategy Nash equilibrium of this version of the model.[13]

PROPOSITION 1: Suppose that the entrants and the incumbent are not permitted to settle their legal disputes and instead must litigate. Then the unique pure strategy Nash equilibrium of the model is a pair of cutoff projects $(\bar{z}_a^* = \bar{z}_l, \bar{z}_b^* = \bar{z}_l)$, where $\bar{z}_l$ satisfies:

(1) $\qquad \pi_E(2)(1-\bar{z}_l)\alpha(1-\alpha F(\bar{z}_l)) - c\int_0^{\bar{z}_l}(1-\alpha F(x))dx = 0$ .

In the Nash equilibrium of the model without settlement, each entrant pursues any project that yields non-negative expected profits. Equation (1) in the proposition is the condition that defines the equilibrium cutoff project $\bar{z}_l$. In the equilibrium, the entrants expect to earn non-negative profits only from projects with completion times that are less than or equal to $\bar{z}_l$. I notice that, in this version of the model, there is some value to being the second entrant to complete its project, even though $\pi_E(3) = 0$. An entrant does not necessarily need to complete its project first in order to profitably enter, since the entrant that completes its project first may lose its infringement case.

---

[13] The proofs of Proposition 1 and all other formal results are located in the Appendix.

Using the entrants' Nash equilibrium strategies, it is straightforward to calculate expected consumer surplus when the incumbent and the entrants cannot settle their legal disputes. Define $CS_n$ as consumer surplus when there are $n \in \{1, 2, \ldots\}$ firms selling in the market. It is reasonable to assume that $CS_{(n+1)} > CS_n$, and I normalize $CS_1$ to be equal to zero. Then expected consumer surplus in the Nash equilibrium given in Proposition 1, say $ECS_l$, is:

$$(2) \qquad ECS_l = CS_2 \int_0^{\bar{z}_l} 2f(x)(1-F(x)) \left[ \alpha(1-x) + \alpha(1-\alpha) \int_x^{\bar{z}_l} \frac{f(y)}{1-F(x)}(1-y)dy \right] dx .$$

In expression (2), the integral represents the expected amount of time that consumers will benefit from an entrant's presence. The bracketed term in the integrand is proportional to the expected surplus that consumers receive when the first entrant to complete its project does so at time $x \leq \bar{z}_l$. This term reflects both the $\alpha$ probability that the first entrant wins its infringement case, in which case consumers benefit from the entrant for $1 - x$ periods, and the $1 - \alpha$ probability that the first entrant loses in court, in which case consumers benefit from entry only if the second entrant also found it worthwhile to start a project. The expectation is taken with respect to the first entrant's completion date, which is distributed according to the probability density function $2f(x)(1 - F(x))$. Entry benefits consumers only if at least one of the entrants initially has a project that it could complete before $\bar{z}_l$. If not, neither entrant starts a project, and there is no entry until the incumbent's patent expires.

I now suppose that the incumbent and the entrants can settle their legal disputes before trial. Permitting settlement bargaining between the firms introduces a degree of indeterminacy into the model, since it is typically not possible to predict the exact division of the surplus that the firms create through an agreement, at least without making somewhat hard-to-justify assumptions about the nature of their bargaining. In this model, any settlement bargaining between the incumbent and the *second* entrant is an exception to this general rule, since the lack of litigation costs and risk aversion means that a settlement between them creates no surplus to divide. The incumbent and the second entrant are therefore both indifferent between litigating and settling for an entry date at time $t_2^* = 1 - \alpha + \alpha z_2$, where $z_2$ is the date on which the second entrant completes its project.[14]

A settlement between the first entrant and the incumbent does potentially create surplus that the litigants can divide, and the division of this surplus affects consumer welfare. The surplus arises in this case because a settlement between the first entrant and the incumbent induces the second entrant to abandon any project it has begun. I begin by identifying the range of possible settlements between the first entrant and the incumbent. To do this, it is necessary to determine the firms' threat points in their settlement bargaining, which depend on their expected payoffs from litigation. Neither the incumbent nor the first entrant would accept a settlement that yielded lower expected profits than it would receive from litigation.

If the first entrant completes its project at time $z_1$, its expected payoff from litigation is $L_E = \alpha \pi_E(2)(1 - z_1)$. This payoff reflects the fact that the entrant wins in court with probability $\alpha$, in which case it earns duopoly profits for $1 - z_1$ periods.

The incumbent's payoff from going to court against the first entrant depends on whether it anticipates that the second entrant might continue developing a project if the first entrant loses in court. If the incumbent believes that the second entrant will not pursue its project, regardless of the outcome of the first entrant's litigation, then the incumbent's payoff from litigation is $L_I = (\alpha \pi_I(2) + (1 - \alpha)\pi_I(1))(1 - z_1)$. It is easy to verify that, in this situation, settlement between the first entrant and the second entrant creates no surplus, and so any settlement would permit entry by the first entrant at time $t_1^* = 1 - \alpha + \alpha z_1$. The more interesting case arises when the incumbent believes that, if the first entrant loses in court, the second entrant will continue developing any project that it can complete before some cutoff date, say $\bar{z}_2 > z_1$. Then the incumbent's expected payoff from litigation against the first entrant is:

---

[14] This settlement reflects the fact that the second entrant has a $1 - \alpha$ chance of losing in court, in which case it can enter after the patent expires at time 1, and an $\alpha$ chance of winning in court, in which case it can enter immediately at time $z_2$.

$L_I =$

$$\alpha(1-z_1)\pi_I(2) +$$

$$(1-\alpha)\left[\frac{(1-F(\bar{z}_2))}{(1-F(z_1))}(1-z_1)\pi_I(1) + \int_{z_1}^{\bar{z}_2}\frac{f(x)}{(1-F(z_1))}(\alpha((x-z_1)\pi_I(1)+(1-x)\pi_I(2))+(1-\alpha)(1-z_1)\pi_I(1)dx\right]$$

$$= \alpha(1-z_1)\pi_I(2) + (1-\alpha)\left[(1-z_1)\pi_I(1) - \int_{z_1}^{\bar{z}_2}\frac{f(x)}{(1-F(z_1))}(\alpha(1-x)(\pi_I(1)-\pi_I(2))dx\right].$$

A settlement between the incumbent and the first entrant specifies a date, say $t_1^* \in [z_1,$ 1], on which the entrant can first sell its product. The entrant's payoff from a settlement is

$$S_E = (1 - t_1^*)\pi_E(2),$$

and the incumbent's payoff is:

$$S_I = (1 - t_1^*)\pi_I(2) + (t_1^* - z_1)\pi_I(1).$$

Using the two parties' payoffs from litigation and settlement, it is straightforward to determine the range of possible settlements that the incumbent and the entrant could reach.[15] If, as is the case in the Nash equilibrium of the model, both entrants pursue any project that can be completed before a common cutoff, say $\bar{z}_s$, then under a settlement the first entrant to complete its

project, say at time $z_1$, will enter the market at a time $t_1^* \in [1 - \alpha + \alpha z_1 - \alpha(1-\alpha)\int_{z_1}^{\bar{z}_s}\frac{f(x)(1-x)}{1-F(z)}dx,$

$1 - \alpha + \alpha z_1]$.

Because my goal is to identify the potentially negative effects of patent settlements on consumers, I assume that the incumbent and the first entrant that completes its project reach the settlement that is most favorable to consumers, subject to the constraint that each firm (at least weakly) prefers the settlement to litigation. If consumers prefer litigation to such a settlement, then, *a fortiori*, they prefer litigation to settlements that are less favorable to their interests. From the perspective of consumers, the best possible settlement involves the earliest possible entry by

---

[15] To find the latest possible entry date that the entrant would accept, set $S_E = L_E$ and solve for $t_1^*$. To find the earliest possible entry date that the incumbent would accept, set $S_I = L_I$ and again solve for $t_1^*$.

one of the two entrants and leaves the incumbent just indifferent between litigating and settling.

There are two reasons for consumers' preference for early entry. First, when entry occurs sooner, consumers receive the incremental consumer surplus that an additional competitor produces for a longer period of time. Second, earlier entry dates enable the entrants to earn greater expected profits, increasing the entrants' incentives to challenge the incumbent's monopoly.[16]

Given the assumption on settlement bargaining, the Nash equilibrium of the model can again be described by a pair of cutoff projects, say $(\bar{z}_a^{**}, \bar{z}_b^{**})$, such that each entrant's choice of a cutoff project maximizes its expected profits given the other entrant's strategy. In the following Proposition, I describe the unique pure strategy Nash equilibrium of this version of the model.

PROPOSITION 2: Suppose that the entrants and the incumbent always settle on the most favorable possible terms for consumers. Then the unique pure strategy Nash equilibrium of the model is a pair of cutoff projects $(\bar{z}_a^{**} = \bar{z}_s, \bar{z}_b^{**} = \bar{z}_s)$, where $\bar{z}_s$ satisfies:

$$(3) \qquad \pi_E(2)(1 - \bar{z}_s)\alpha(1 - F(\bar{z}_s)) - c\int_0^{\bar{z}_s}(1 - F(x))dx = 0.$$

As in the version of the model without settlement, each entrant pursues any project that yields non-negative expected profits, i.e. any project with a completion time that is less than or equal to $\bar{z}_s$. A key difference between the two versions of the model, however, is that, with settlement, there is no value to being the second entrant to complete its project. Because the first entrant and the incumbent always settle on terms that eventually allow the first entrant to sell its product, the second entrant always stops work on its project after the first entrant settles with the incumbent.

---

[16] This discussion reflects consumers' interests with respect to entry by the two hypothesized entrants only. It specifically sets aside consumers' interest with respect to providing the incumbent with an incentive to develop its patented good in the first place.

Using the entrants' Nash equilibrium strategies, it is straightforward to calculate expected consumer surplus when the incumbent and the entrants settle their legal disputes on the terms that are most favorable to consumers. Expected consumer surplus, say $ECS_s$, is:

$$(4) \qquad ECS_s = CS_2 \int_0^{\bar{z}_s} 2f(x)(1-F(x)) \left[ \alpha(1-x) + \alpha(1-\alpha) \int_x^{\bar{z}_s} \frac{f(y)}{1-F(x)}(1-y)dy \right] dx .$$

In expression (4), the integral represents the expected amount of time that consumers will benefit from an entrant. If an entrant completes its project at a time $x \le \bar{z}_s$, the earliest entry date that the incumbent will accept is $t^*(x) = 1 - \alpha + \alpha x - \alpha(1-\alpha) \int_x^{\bar{z}_s} \frac{f(y)(1-y)}{1-F(x)} dy$, so under the assumption about bargaining, consumers benefit from the entrant for $1 - t^*(x)$ periods. I notice that, except for the entrants' cutoff project ($\bar{z}_s$ rather than $\bar{z}_l$), the expression for expected consumer surplus given in (4) is identical to the expression for expected consumer surplus when the firms always litigate, given in (2).

The following lemma helps to address the issue of how settlement affects consumers. It establishes that the entrants are less likely to start developing a product when settlement is possible, compared to when they always litigate their cases.

LEMMA 1: Each entrant is less likely to start a project when settlement is possible, compared to when they must litigate their cases, i.e. $\bar{z}_s \le \bar{z}_l$.

When settlement is not possible, an entrant need not be the first to finish its project in order to enter, even though it would never enter as a triopolist. The firm that is second to finish its project may enter the market because the firm that is first to finish may lose its infringement case. When the incumbent and the first entrant can settle their infringement case, on the other hand, there is no value to being the second entrant, because the first entrant will always settle and (eventually) enter the market. When settlement is possible, it is not profitable to start a project that will take a relatively long time to finish, because the odds of being the first to finish are relatively low.

Obviously, this result depends to some extent on the assumption that litigation costs are zero. If litigation costs are significant and settlement is not possible, an entrant may have little incentive to try to invent around the incumbent's patent. But the maintained assumption that the entrant captures the entire surplus under settlement bargaining is extreme as well, and it serves to increase the incentive to invent around the incumbent's patent when settlement is possible. A more realistic division of the bargaining surplus between the incumbent and the entrant would further depress the entrants' incentives to invest when settlement is possible.

The following proposition contains the main result.

PROPOSITION 3: Expected consumer surplus is lower when the incumbent and the entrants can settle their patent infringement cases, compared to when they must litigate, i.e. $ECS_s <$ $ECS_l$.

The proposition establishes that, even when settlements between the incumbent and the entrants are on terms that are most favorable to consumers, consumers are still better off if the firms litigate their cases rather than settle. This result stems from the fact that, in this model, the entrants are less likely to develop a competing product and challenge the incumbent's monopoly when they can settle an infringement case. Consumers would be even worse off under a settlement if the incumbent and the entrants agreed to terms that enabled the incumbent to capture part of the surplus that a settlement with the first entrant creates.

## 4.    Discussion and Conclusions

My analysis employs several simplifying assumptions. Because they may not always be satisfied, I conclude by discussing how my conclusions might depend on some of them. The assumption that litigation is costless is clearly not realistic. Litigation imposes direct costs on the parties (e.g. attorney fees, the opportunity cost of time spent on case preparation, etc.), and, if the parties are risk averse, the uncertainty of the trial's outcome also imposes a cost. There are two ways that such litigation costs could influence the analysis. First, they could affect the terms of any settlement. If, for example, incumbents typically bear far greater litigation costs than entrants, including litigation costs in the analysis could possibly swing the terms of settlement more in the entrants' (and consumers') favor, offsetting the conclusion that, at least in the natural duopoly model, consumers are harmed by settlements.

Second, to the extent that litigation costs are avoided with settlement and not avoided if the parties litigate their cases, ignoring them tends to bias the comparison of a settlement regime and a litigation regime in favor of the litigation regime, unless the incumbent captures the lion's share of the surplus created by settlement. The reason is that litigation costs increase a potential entrant's cost of bringing a product to market, reducing the incentive to try to invent around the incumbent's patent. Whether this effect is great enough to reverse the conclusions given in the paper depends on how significant litigation costs are relative to the expected profits that an entrant expects to earn. In situations where these costs are relatively small, or if the entrant receives a sufficiently small fraction of the surplus created by bargaining, the conclusion that consumers prefer for the firms to litigate will still hold.

My model also reflects an assumption that the two entrants' cases are statistically independent. There may be circumstances where it would be more appropriate to assume that the entrants' cases are correlated. For example, the entrants may have adopted similar strategies to invent around the incumbent's patent.[17] Suppose that the entrants' cases were perfectly correlated. Then settlement between the incumbent and the first entrant deprives the second entrant of information about its case. Because the second entrant would enter at best as a triopolist, it might not continue its project without knowing whether it would win. If a settlement between the first entrant and the incumbent deters entry that would follow a win by the first

---

[17] If the entrants alleged that the incumbent's patent were invalid, rather than merely not infringed by their products, then their cases would be correlated.

entrant in court, both benefit from the external effect of settlement. On the other hand, if settlement is not possible, the entrants' cases are correlated, and litigation costs are significant, both entrants may wish to delay their entry and litigation in order to free ride on the information that its rival's litigation would reveal. In this case the entrants' rivalry could lead to a waiting game, as in Choi (1999), and settlement could speed entry. This sort of effect would be particularly pronounced if the entrants litigated the validity of the incumbent's patent, rather than merely asserting that their products did not infringe.

My model also reflects an assumption that the entrants' product development options are exogenous. In some situations, they may be able to choose how to try to invent around the incumbent's patent. For instance, an entrant may have some control over how "close" in the relevant characteristic space to develop a product.[18] By developing a "closer" product, the entrant can presumably complete its work faster and at lower cost, but it also presumably faces a higher probability of being found to infringe the incumbent's patent. The entrants may approach this tradeoff differently depending on whether they can settle any patent infringement suits or instead must litigate. If the ability to settle their legal disputes encourages entrants to develop substitute products faster and at lower cost, then consumers may prefer settlement to litigation.

Finally, I observe that it would be inappropriate to interpret the results of the formal model as implying that settlements of patent disputes routinely harm consumer interests. Rather, the analysis indicates that simple rules of thumb about what kinds of settlements will harm or promote consumer interests may sometimes, or even often, be misleading. Of course, a conceptually simple rule of thumb, e.g. that a patent dispute settlement should reflect the expect outcome of the litigation in question, may be difficult to implement in practice because of the unavailability of the necessary evidence. The analysis in this paper shows that such simple rules may also be wrong.

---

[18] For an example of a model in which entrants must choose where to locate in a product space, see Waterson (1990).

This paper represents at best a first step in the analysis of the antitrust issues that surround the settlement of patent disputes, but it is a first step on an important road. Because settlement is such a key part of any litigation, antitrust policy towards patent settlements has a significant effect on the nature of the property right that a patent represents. The development of a sound basis for this policy is of great importance.

**APPENDIX**

*Proof of Proposition 1:* I first notice that $H(z) = \pi_E(2)(1-z)\alpha(1-\alpha F(z)) - c\int_0^z (1-\alpha F(x))dx$
is a continuous, monotone decreasing function of $z$, and $H(0) > 0 > H(1)$. Therefore, there exists a unique $\bar{z}_l$ satisfying $H(\bar{z}_l) = 0$. Suppose that entrant $i$ believes that $j$ is choosing a cutoff $\bar{z}_l$. Entrant $i$ pursues any project that yields non-negative profit, and its net profit from pursuing a project with $z \leq \bar{z}_l$ is $H(z)$; the first term in $H(\cdot)$ reflects the fact that the entrant earns duopoly profits for $(1-z)$ periods if both it wins its patent litigation and the other entrant has not already completed its project and prevailed in its patent litigation, and the second term reflects the entrant's expected cost of pursuing the project, adjusted to reflect the possibility that its rival will finish first. But then entrant $i$'s best reply to entrant $j$ choosing a cutoff $\bar{z}_l$ is to choose the same cutoff itself, and there is a unique symmetric pure strategy Nash Equilibrium in which both entrants choose $\bar{z}_l$. It remains to show that there does not exist an asymmetric pure strategy Nash Equilibrium. Assume without loss of generality that $\bar{z}_1 < \bar{z}_2$. Because entrant 1's payoff from a project with $z \leq \bar{z}_2$ is $H(z)$, it follows immediately that $\bar{z}_1 = \bar{z}_l$. But entrant 2's payoff from a project with $z > \bar{z}_l$ is $\pi_E(2)(1-z)\alpha(1-\alpha F(\bar{z}_l)) - c\int_0^z (1-\alpha F(x))dx < H(\bar{z}_l) = 0$, so it is not optimal for entrant 2 to choose a cutoff $\bar{z}_2 > \bar{z}_l$, and there exists no asymmetric pure strategy Nash Equilibrium. QED

*Proof of Proposition 2:* Suppose that entrant $i$ believes that entrant $j$ is choosing a cutoff $\bar{z}_s$. Then arguments identical to those in the proof of Proposition 1 establish that $\bar{z}_s$ is also entrant $i$'s best reply, substituting $G(z) = \pi_E(2)(1-z)\alpha(1-F(z)) - c\int_0^z (1-F(x))dx$ for $H(z)$ and recognizing that the settlement that the incumbent and first entrant reach at time $z_1 = \bar{z}_s$ is for the first entrant to enter at $1 - \alpha + \alpha\bar{z}_s$. It remains to show that there does not exist an asymmetric pure strategy Nash equilibrium. Assume without loss of generality that $\bar{z}_a < \bar{z}_b$. In an asymmetric equilibrium, the settlement between the incumbent and the entrant will depend on the identity of the entrant. Under the assumption that the entrant captures all of the surplus from bargaining, the incumbent's settlement with entrant $a$ permits entry at time $t_a^*(x) = 1 - \alpha + \alpha z_a - \alpha(1-\alpha)\int_{z_a}^{\bar{z}_b} \frac{f(y)(1-y)}{1-F(x)}dy$, $z_a \leq \bar{z}_a$. The incumbent's settlement with entrant $b$ permits entry at time:

$$t_b^*(z_b) = \begin{cases} 1 - \alpha + \alpha z_b - \alpha(1-\alpha)\int_{z_b}^{\bar{z}_a} \frac{f(y)(1-y)}{1-F(z_b)}dy, z_b \leq \bar{z}_a \\ 1 - \alpha + \alpha z_b, z_b > \bar{z}_a \end{cases}.$$

For $\bar{z}_a$ to be a best reply for entrant a, its payoff from a project with a completion date exactly equal to $\bar{z}_a$ must be equal to zero, i.e.

$$(A1)\ \pi_E(2)(\alpha(1-\bar{z}_a) + \alpha(1-\alpha)\int_{\bar{z}_a}^{\bar{z}_b} \frac{f(x)(1-x)}{1-F(\bar{z}_a)}dx)(1-F(\bar{z}_a)) - c\int_0^{\bar{z}_a} (1-F(x))dx = 0.$$

But entrant $b$'s payoff from pursuing any project with a completion date $z > \bar{z}_a$ is:

$$(A2)\ \pi_E(2)\alpha(1-z)(1-F(\bar{z}_a)) - c(\int_0^{\bar{z}_a} (1-F(x))dx + (1-F(\bar{z}_a))(z-\bar{z}_a))$$

which is strictly less than entrant $a$'s payoff in (A1) and is therefore negative. It immediately follows that entrant $b$ does not wish to choose a cutoff $\bar{z}_b > \bar{z}_a$, and there exists no asymmetric pure strategy Nash equilibrium. QED

*Proof of Lemma* 1: Define $I(m,z) = \pi_E(2)(1-z)\alpha(1-mF(z)) - c\int_0^z(1-mF(x))dx$. $I(m,z) \equiv 0$ implicitly defines a function $z(m)$ on the domain [0, 1]. I notice that $z(\alpha) = \bar{z}_l$, and $z(1) = \bar{z}_s$. Because $\alpha < 1$, it is sufficient to show that $z' < 0$. Using the Implicit Function Theorem, I have:

$$(A3) \qquad z' = \frac{-\partial I / \partial m}{\partial I / \partial z} = \frac{-F(z)\alpha\pi_E(2)(1-z) + c\int_0^z F(x)dx}{(\pi_E(2)\alpha + c)(1-mF(z))}.$$

Because the denominator in (A3) is greater than zero on the relevant domain, $z' < 0$ if and only if $-F(z)\alpha\pi_E(2)(1-z) + c\int_0^z F(x)dx < 0$. Because $F(x) < F(z)$ for $x \leq z$, it is sufficient to show that $\alpha\pi_E(2)(1-z) > cz$. Because $I(m,z) \equiv 0$, it follows that $\alpha\pi_E(2)(1-z) = c\int_0^z \frac{1-mF(x)}{1-mF(z)}dx > cz$, which establishes the result.

QED

*Proof of Proposition 3*: Define

$$ECS(z) = CS_2 \int_0^z 2f(x)(1-F(x))\left[\alpha(1-x) + \alpha(1-\alpha)\int_x^z \frac{f(y)}{1-F(x)}(1-y)dy\right]dx.$$

Simple differentiation establishes that $dECS/dz > 0$, and the result follows immediately from the Lemma, which establishes that $\bar{z}_s \leq \bar{z}_l$.

QED

# REFERENCES

Choi, Jay Pil (1998). "Patent Litigation as an Information-Transmission Mechanism," *American Economic Review*, **88:** 1249 – 1263.

Hovenkamp, Herbert et al. (2003). "Anticompetitive Settlement of Intellectual Property Disputes," *Minnesota Law Review*, 87:1719.

Meurer, Michael J. (1989). "The Settlement of Patent Litigation," *RAND Journal of Economics*, **20:** 77 – 91.

O'Rourke, Maureen and Joseph Brodley (2003). "Antitrust Implications of Patent Settlements: An Incentives Modifying Approach," *Minnesota Law Review*, 87: 101.

Schrag, Joel (2004). "An Antitrust Gordian Knot: Analyzing the Competitive Effects of Patent Settlements," unpublished manuscript.

Shapiro, Carl (2003). "Antitrust Limits to Patent Settlements," *RAND Journal of Economics*, 34:391.

Shapiro, Carl and Mark Lemley (2005). "Probabilistic Patents," *Journal of Economic Perspectives*, 19: 75 - 98.

Waterson, Michael (1990), "The Economics of Product Patents," *American Economic Review*, **80:**860 – 869.